About us

Our mission is to provide equal service to individuals of all ages, cultures, and backgrounds, while fostering the inherent creativity within each individual. Through the release of our coloring books and creations, our company is dedicated to engaging our customers in activities that promote cognitive development, alleviate stress and anxiety, nurture spirituality, and achieve numerous other benefits.

Belongs _______________

Accomplish

Believe

Create

Determine

Empower

Fearless

Goal

Hope

Inspire

Joyful

Know

Lead

Mindset

Nurture

Optimistic

Persist

Qualified

Reach

Succeed

Trustworthy

Understand

Value

Willpower

Xenacious

Yes

Zen

www.ingramcontent.com/pod-product-compliance
Lightning Source LLC
Chambersburg PA
CBHW080850250726
48663CB00003B/407